C000055759

INSTRUMENTS

ASHMOLEAN HANDBOOKS

STRINGED INSTRUMENTS

VIOLS, VIOLINS, CITTERNS, AND GUITARS
IN THE ASHMOLEAN MUSEUM

JON WHITELEY

ASHMOLEAN

Stringed Instruments: Viols, Violins, Citterns and Guitars in the Ashmolean Museum

Copyright © Ashmolean Museum, University of Oxford, 2008
Reprinted 2013

Jon Whiteley has asserted his moral right to be identified as the
author of this work.

British Library Cataloguing in Publications Data

A catalogue record for this book is available from the British Library

EAN 13: 978 1 85444 200 0 (paperback) (ISBN: 1 85444 200 7)
EAN 13: 978 1 85444 199 7 (hardback) (ISBN: 1 85444 199 X)

All rights reserved. No part of this publication may be transmitted
in any form or by any means, electronic or mechanical, including
photocopy, recording or any storage and retrieval system, without
the prior permission in writing of the publisher.

OTHER TITLES AVAILABLE:
Ruskin's Drawings
Worcester Porcelain
Oxford and the Pre-Raphaelites
Drawings by Michelangelo and Raphael
Camille Pissarro and his Family
Eighteenth-Century French Porcelain
Samuel Palmer
Twentieth-Century Paintings
J.M.W. Turner Watercolours and Drawings
English Delftware
French Drawings and Watercolours
Frames and Framing
Italian Maiolica
English Embroideries

Designed and typeset in Aldus by Geoff Green
Printed and bound in Great Britain by Henry Ling Ltd, Dorchester

For further details of these or any of these titles please visit:
www.ashmolean.org/shop

Contents

Introduction

The Ashmolean's collection of European stringed instruments is not large but it is very famous. Several of the instruments in the Ashmolean are among the rarest and most beautiful of their kind, and most are, in some way, exceptional. The collection was founded on a group of instruments that was given to the museum by the firm of W. E. Hill & Sons in 1939, with further gifts from Arthur Hill, Alfred Hill, and A. Phillips Hill in 1940, 1946, and 1948. The collection has since been increased by two bequests and by an important group of bows and instruments given by Albert Cooper in 1999, but it remains, in essence, the Hill Collection, a select group of early stringed instruments, mostly by Italian makers, formed by the Hill family in the late nineteenth and early twentieth centuries.

The firm of W. E. Hill & Sons was founded in 1880 by William Ebsworth Hill (1817–95), great-great-grandson of Joseph Hill (1715–84), the first known violin-maker in the family. By the early twentieth century, the firm had achieved an unrivalled reputation in making, restoring, and selling stringed instruments. A large number of important historic instruments passed through their hands, many of which were skilfully and sympathetically restored by William Ebsworth Hill and his assistants in the firm's workshops. In the course of handling and repairing instruments, the Hills became increasingly aware of the damage that was being inflicted on early viols and violins by constant playing and repeated restoration. This concern gave rise to the idea of donating a select group of rare instruments to a museum where they would be preserved from further harm. In 1936 William Ebsworth's sons, Arthur and

Alfred, began discussions with the Ashmolean, and the first instruments were handed over in 1939. Progress in creating a gallery for the collection was delayed by the war, and it was not installed in a room of its own until 1950.

David Boyden's catalogue of the Hill Collection, first published in 1969, has been out of print for many years*. The present handbook discusses and illustrates every stringed instrument in the collection, but it is not intended to be a substitute for Boyden's book. A new, comprehensive catalogue, edited by John Milnes with contributions by John Dilworth and others, is in hand. This will provide the scholarly detail that the specialist will expect. The student of the subject, meanwhile, may find some use in this handbook, but it is chiefly intended for the many visitors to the Hill Collection and for the wider public who might wish for more information about the instruments and some back-ground history.

The author is grateful to Stephen Barber, Charles Beare, John Dilworth, Michael Fleming, Fritz Grahl, Colin Harrison, Kate Heard, Andrew and David Hill, John Milnes, Stewart Pollens, John Topham, and Linda Whiteley. He is particularly grateful to Ben Hebbert for many discussions about the instruments, to Stephen Harris and Ray Ansty for identifying the woods, and to John Dilworth and Michael Fleming for suggesting many improvements to the text.

*Since this book was first published, a new catalogue of the Hill Collection of Musical Instruments has been produced (*Musical Instruments in the Ashmolean Museum*, edited by John Milnes, 2010).

Note on the Text

'Boyden' refers to David Boyden, *The Hill Collection* (Oxford, 1969; 2nd edn., 1979); 'Cooper' refers to Albert Cooper, *The Cooper Collection*, 2 vols. (Ashford, 1996, 1998); 'Topham', followed by a date, refers to the date of the latest tree ring identified by John Topham in a dendrochronological analysis of the softwood fronts undertaken in 1998 and published in the *Galpin Society Journal*, 55 (Apr. 2002), 244–68.

All measurements are given in millimetres.

Detailed working drawings of selected instruments in the Hill Collection can be purchased from The Publications Department, Ashmolean Museum, Beaumont Street, Oxford OX1 2PH. The following are available: Boyden 1–8, 10–13, 15, 17, 18, 31–3, 40, 41.

1. Viols

The idea of making music by plucking a string fixed to a soundbox is very old. The ancient Egyptians, Assyrians, and Greeks had harps, lyres, and instruments with long necks that were played by plucking. Bowed instruments are a more recent invention. There is no evidence that the bow was used for making music before the ninth century, when some musician in the Arab world first drew a bow across the strings of his instrument and produced a new, prolonged, resonating sound. This use of the bow led to the development of the Arab rebab, a pear-shaped instrument with a long neck, and to its offshoot, the mediaeval rebec, a small three-stringed instrument that seems to have played a part in the history of all later European bowed instruments.

It is generally believed that the viol developed in late fifteenth-century Spain when the the bow was applied to the medieval vihuela. Few viols survive before *c.*1550, but viol-playing angels and other viol-playing musicians appear in many fifteenth- and sixteenth-century prints and paintings. The earliest evidence of viols is found in paintings from Valencia of the 1470s and 80s, which feature angels playing instruments with fretted necks and indented middle bouts, characteristic of the early viol, held downwards, either on the lap or between the legs: hence 'viola da gamba' (leg-viol), as the viols are generally called. It has been suggested that Pope Alexander VI, who came from Valencia, may have been partly responsible for bringing the viol to Rome and, perhaps, to Urbino and Ferrara, cities with close links to the papacy. Before the end of the century, Isabella d'Este, sister of Alfonso, Duke of Ferrara, had brought the viol to Mantua, and it was rapidly taken up throughout Italy and the rest of Europe as a courtly

instrument, played by professionals in consort, but also by aristocrats and other wealthy amateurs.

By the middle of the sixteenth century, the viol had acquired its typical features: a deep soundbox, a flat back with an inward sloping upper part, and an arched bridge and fingerboard. The viol normally has six strings, attached at the lower end to a tailpiece, which is rigidly fixed to an upright post or 'hookbar' set into the lower rib. By contrast, the tailpiece of the violin and of the other members of the violin family is flexibly mounted by means of a gut loop passing over the lower edge and around a small peg inserted into the rib.

Bologna, Brescia, and Venice, North Italian towns close to plentiful supplies of Alpine spruce and pine, became the major centres for the production of Italian viols, whereas in Cremona, the Amati family concentrated on making violins. It was the triumph of the violin family at the end of the sixteenth century that ousted the viol in Italy. In England, where viol-players were first employed at the court of Henry VIII, it remained in fashion throughout the seventeenth century, encouraged by its use in choir schools and by the wealth of music written for it by Orlando Gibbons, John Jenkins, William Lawes, and others. Because of this, England became a centre for the production of high-quality viols. Beautiful viols were also made in eighteenth-century France, and, while the smaller treble and tenor viols passed from fashion, the bass viol remained in common use as a solo instrument. The major repertoire for the solo bass viol in France and elsewhere dates from the eighteenth century. It was not, however, well adapted to deal with the music of the nineteenth century, and, because of this, it was universally passed over in favour of the violin, the viola, and the cello.

Treble viol by Giovanni Maria of Brescia (working c.1560–c.1590)

Label printed in red: *Zuan Maria da Bressa: / fece in Venecia.*

Length with neck: 622; length of body: 358; width of upper, middle, and lower bouts: 178, 137, 215; max. depth of sides: 70; string length: 314

Boyden, no. 1
Presented by W. E. Hill & Sons, 1939

This stout little instrument is a rare survival of a once common type of sixteenth-century viol. The ball-like scroll with flat sides, the short neck, the thickish finger-board, the guitar-shaped soundbox, and the flat back with an inward sloping upper section are common features, which can be matched in a number of Venetian paintings and prints of the period. It is in remarkably unrestored condition for an instrument of its age. The pegs are modern, but the neck, the fingerboard, the pegbox, and, possibly, the tailpiece are original. The front is made of a fairly open-grained spruce, and the sides and back are made of maple. At one time, the maker was identified as the father of Giovanni Giacobo dalla Corna of Brescia, who lived from about 1485 to about 1550. Had this been true, the viol would have been astonishingly early. It is now known that this Giovanni Maria da Brescia worked in Venice in the later sixteenth century and could not have been Giovanni Giacobo's father. The label is printed in a Rotunda type, which, according to Boyden, was not used after c.1560. But Giovanni Maria no doubt had a stock of labels that he used over a period of years. The use of a label with a more fashionable type in a lira da braccio, also in the Ashmolean (see p. 32), might, however, suggest that this viol dates from an earlier stage in his career.

Bass viol by Gasparo da Salò (1540–1609)

Printed label: *Gaspar da Salò in Brescia*

Length with neck: 1,163; length of body: 680; width of upper, middle, and lower bouts: 337, 232, 420; max. depth of sides: 133; string length: 642

Boyden, no. 2
Presented by W. E. Hill & Sons, 1939

Gasparo Bertolotti took the name Gasparo da Salò from the town of Salò on Lake Garda, where he was born in 1540. He is said to have moved to Brescia in about 1562, where he became one of the leading members of the flourishing Brescian school of makers of stringed instruments. This instrument has several features that are typical of the sixteenth-century viol: the tailpiece, mounted on a hook bar, the sloping upper back, the indented middle bouts with pointed corners, and the c-shaped sound holes with central nicks. The ball-like scroll with a single central flute is an early variant of the scroll head in its more familiar form. The three-lobed gothic rose is placed over a strengthening bar, which cuts across the opening. The front is made of spruce, strongly marked by a lattice-pattern grain, while the back and sides are made of maple. The finger-board is original, but the tailpiece, made to match the fingerboard, is later. The neck is also original but has been damaged and repaired where it joins the body. A letter A is scratched onto the top of the tailpeg. The join between the ribs along the front and back is reinforced with a strip of moulding, cut into sections to fit the curve in the upper back. It is a robust instrument, boldly designed, sharing some features in common with the following viol. Both instruments have squarish fronts, neatly arched, with sharp ridges that rise out-wards from the corners, deep inward curving middle bouts, and a rose placed high in the middle of the upper bouts. This is a type of viol, found elsewhere in north-ern Italy, that may also have been made in Spain or for the Spanish market. A similar viol appears in El Greco's

Annunciation, painted between 1596 and 1600 for the Colegio de Dona Maria de Aragón in Madrid (Museo Balaguer), and it may be significant that the Ashmolean viol belonged, at one time, to Burgos cathedral.

Bass viol by Dominico Russo (late sixteenth century)

Length with neck: 1,105; length of body: 604; width of upper, middle, and lower bouts: 349, 219, 407; max. depth of sides: 146; string length: 613

Boyden, no. 3
Presented by W. E. Hill & Sons, 1939

The shape is similar to Gasparo's bass viol, with ridges extending from the bout corners onto the belly and a rose hole set high on the belly between the upper bouts. The outline is squarish, almost dumpy, but the spruce front is elegantly shaped, with flat arching, and a band of purfling (a strip of pale wood sandwiched between two black strips) is inlaid along the contours. The back is flat, canted at the shoulders, and made of dark figured walnut, without purfling. The neck, fingerboard, and tailpiece are new, but the elaborately carved pegbox and head, grafted onto the neck, are original. The pegbox is decorated with foliate scrolls and ends in a finely carved satyr's head. This characteristic Renaissance ornament is combined with a gilt sunken rose and eleven diamond-shaped insets on the front inlaid with pale wood, white and green-stained bone or ivory, and black mastic. Remarkably, a twin to the Ashmolean viol, now converted to a cello, survives in the Tiroler Landesmuseum Ferdinandeum in Innsbruck, boldly inscribed *Dominico Russo* on the paper label. Various attempts to identify this maker have been made, including the suggestion that he might be a Dominico who made keyboard instruments for the Spanish court. This is tempting, because similar insets of coloured wood and bone reappear on an early Spanish guitar in the Jacquemart-André Museum in Paris. All three instruments were perhaps made in the same late sixteenth-century workshop. Was this a Spanish workshop? The inlay has a distinctly Spanish character. On the other hand, a similar inlaid viol appears in Giovanni Serodine's *Coronation of the Virgin* in the parish church of

Ascona, a town north-west of Brescia, too far, perhaps, to make a link with Brescia certain, but indicating that viols of this type were known in the seventeenth century within reach of at least one of the great centres of instrument-making in northern Italy.

Bass viol by the brothers Amati: Antonio (c.1540–1607) and Girolamo (c.1561–1630)

As David Boyden points out, this is a viol that looks somewhat like a cello. The back is carved like the back of instruments of the violin family, but similar backs, as Michael Fleming has pointed out, are not uncommonly found in viols, especially in late seventeenth- and early eighteenth-century Germany. It has, in addition, the broad neck and sloping upper back of the typical viol, and a pegbox made for six strings. As the neck is a replacement, one cannot be certain that the pegbox now grafted onto the neck is the original, but it appears to be an authentic Amati pegbox of the period. The front is made from two pieces of spruce, joined at the centre, as is normal, but extended in the lower bouts by a piece added to each side. In common with most of the instruments from the workshop of the Amati brothers, this one has a label attributing it to both Antonio and Girolamo, although Girolamo bought out his brother's share of the firm in 1588, and all instruments after this date were probably made by Girolamo or under his supervision. Antonio, who was twenty years older than his brother, died in 1607, confirming that Girolamo was solely responsible for the workshop when the Ashmolean viol was made. The button is branded with a letter M, which has been associated, on slender grounds, with the Medici family. There is a similar viol from the Amati workshop, bearing the same initial, in the Moscow Conservatoire, and the brand is found again on a viola dated 1592 in the Ashmolean (see p. 38). These were probably part of a sequence of instruments commissioned from the Amatis, the first of

Printed label: *Antonius & Hierony-mus fr. Amat [...] / Cremonen Andreae fil. F. 1611* (the date added in pen and ink)

Length with neck: 1,099; length of body: 629; width of upper, middle, and lower bouts: 327, 216, 400; max. depth of sides: 102; string length: 460

Boyden, no. 7
Presented by W. E. Hill & Sons, 1939

which was made in the lifetime of Andrea Amati, father
of the brothers and founder of the famous workshop.

Small tenor viol by Richard Blunt (late sixteenth–early seventeenth century)

Length with neck: 1,048; length of body: 578; width of upper, middle, and lower bouts: 268, 192, 322; max. depth of sides: 105; string length: 587

Boyden, no. 6
Presented by W. E. Hill & Sons, 1939

This is a classic English viol with characteristic tapering shoulders, a front assembled from five lengths of spruce, joined along the grain, and inlaid with double purfling. The sides and two-piece back are made of maple, and the sides are fitted to the front and back without an overhang. The c-holes are broad and slightly asymmetrical. The neck and fingerboard are not original, but the fingerboard is based on an authentic type. The back and sides are undecorated apart from the purfling, but the cheeks and back of the pegbox are ornamented with a typical foliate design, carved in light relief against a ground that has been patterned with a metal punch. The bearded head, with flowing locks, wearing a classical wreath, is vigorously chiselled and is possibly original. When this viol was in the collection of a Miss Oliphant in 1914, it had a label inscribed: *Richard Blunt / dwelling in London / in Fetter Lane 1605*. This is no longer in the instrument. It has been attributed at various times to William Baker of Oxford, John Shaw (with a question mark), and Richard Blanke, and was finally restored to Blunt when the description of the original label came to light. The attribution to Blunt, about whom almost nothing is known, seems more plausible than the others. The viol is said to have belonged to the painter John Constable.

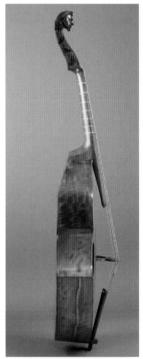

Small tenor viol by John Rose (d. 1611)

Label in pen and ink: *Iohn Rose / 1598*

Length with neck: 1,055; length of body: 587; width of upper, middle, and lower bouts: 253, 180, 323; max. depth of sides: 114; string length: 591

Topham, 1864
Boyden, no. 5
Presented by W. E. Hill & Sons, 1939

There were two instrument-makers called John Rose, a father who is thought to have died in 1563, leaving a son of the same name 'far excelling himself in making Bandores, Voyall de Gamboes and other instruments'. In 1561 John Rose (presumably the father) was granted a lease on premises in Bridewell in London. The ten or so surviving instruments attributed to John Rose are thought to be the work of the more famous son. The label in the Ashmolean viol is written in a hand not dissimilar to the handwriting on an undated label inscribed 'Iohn Rose' in a viol in the Victoria and Albert Museum. The maple back and sides are finely inlaid with a pattern of geometric bands of a kind found on English viols throughout the seventeenth century. The front (as the dendrochronology confirmed) was inserted by W. E. Hill & Sons before 1900. The previous front was presumably in irretrievably bad repair or had been thoroughly altered. The hook-bar, pegs, neck, finger-board, and tailpiece are all new, and, while the pegbox appears to be essentially of the right date, it was, at one time, almost one-third shorter than it now is, and is unlikely to have been made for this viol. The tapering extension grafted onto the pegbox continues the scrolling designs in low relief against a ground that is pricked, not punched as on the original. The fine head of a bearded man, painted black with gilded hair and red lips, does not belong to the present pegbox, but has been sawn off another instrument, somewhat carelessly, as there is a saw cut across the beard. In its present form, the instrument is an attractive confection, incorporating a substantial part of a viol that carries the signature of one of the most famous and rare of English makers.

Bass viol, English, early seventeenth century

Length with neck: 1,298; length of body: 706; width of upper, middle, and lower bouts: 320, 255, 400; max. depth of sides: 122; string length: 740

Topham, 1556
Boyden, no. 4
Presented by W. E. Hill & Sons, 1939

The lively outline of this viol, with its matching flame-like sound-holes, is found on bass viols well into the seventeenth century. It is an exceptionally magnificent instrument, decorated with a complex inlaid knot pattern on the back and sides and with a pattern of leaves and tendrils on the front. The tendrils are inlaid with very narrow stringing, and the leaves have been cross-hatched with a red-hot needle. The arms with the portcullis crest, painted on the front, are those of Sir Charles Somerset (*c.*1585–*c.*1665), from the family of the Dukes of Beaufort. As is typical of English viols, the front is made of five lengths of softwood and inlaid with double purfling. The back and sides, made from a burr wood carefully chosen for its rich pattern, is varnished dark brown. The fingerboard and neck are not original. The pretty pegbox and head have been almost invisibly grafted onto the neck, and have been removed from what must have been an exceptionally fine eighteenth-century French viol. The arms on the pegbox (a fess between three trefoils slipped) have not been identified. The history of the instrument from the time of Sir Charles Somerset until 1929, when it was bought by Alfred Hill from Señor de Landechio in Madrid, is not known. Although there is no label, the viol has been attributed to John Rose the younger. The rose, carved in relief on the highly ornamented hook-bar, may be significant, but it is not certain that the hook-bar is original, and one must be cautious in coming to conclusions when so little of Rose's work survives for comparison.

2. The Violin Family

The violin evolved in northern Italy from earlier Italian stringed instruments a few years after the arrival of the Spanish viol. In the absence of surviving instruments from this period, the evidence comes mainly from prints and paintings in which instruments resembling violins appear from the early 1500s onwards. Like the early rebec, which fell from grace in the late 1500s, or the lira da braccio with which the violin coexisted for many years, these violin-like instruments were played under the chin or held against the chest. They generally had three strings, tuned in fifths like the rebec, without frets, combined with a soundbox shaped like that of the lira da braccio. Unlike earlier types of bowed instruments, which often had a flat bridge or no bridge at all, they were fitted with an arched bridge for polyphonic playing. Instruments of this description are mentioned in contemporary documents and published sources. Jambe de Fer's *Epitome musical*, published in Lyon in 1556, describes it as an instrument for use at dances and other festivities, similar in shape to the viol, but, unlike the viol, which was played by 'gentlemen, merchants, and other persons of culture', the violin was mainly used by professionals. This was published only eight years before Andrea Amati labelled the violin in the Ashmolean, made for the court of Charles IX of France, no doubt at the instigation of the king's mother, Catherine de' Medici. Although this is the earliest dated violin in existence, it is astonishingly similar to the modern instrument. The front is made of close-grained spruce, an ideal resonating softwood, while the sides and back are made of harder maple. Back and front overhang the sides, and a line of purfling decorates the edges. This line may have originated as a decorative feature, but it also has a use in preventing damage on the edge from spreading across the front or back. C-shaped indentations on both sides (the middle bouts), ending in sharp beak-like corners, provide space for the bow to reach the highest and the lowest strings with ease. The sound-holes are cut in the classic f-shape, neatly matching the contours of the middle bouts. Both front and back arch outwards in an elegant wave-like curve, essential for strengthening the soundbox against the high tension of the strings, but also for giving the violin its characteristically expressive sound. The bridge supporting the strings transmits the vibration in the strings to the soundbox. A small post of spruce or pine, inserted inside the soundbox near the bridge on the right, joining top to bottom, provides support but also transmits and harmonizes the vibrations from front to back. A short bar of spruce or pine, known as the bass bar, glued along the inside of the upper plate below the g string, helps to transmit the low-frequency vibrations from the string to the body but also provides essential reinforcement. It has four strings, the highest tuned on the right (the 'treble side'), the lowest on the left (the 'bass side'). The violin is a beautiful object, but it is also highly functional. It is this, above all, that has ensured the undying success of the Amati model down to our own times.

The power of the violin is one of its advantages over the viol in playing festive music. The arching of the front and back, which contributes to the sweetness of the tone, tends, however, to dampen the volume. Over the next century and a half, Andrea's sons, Antonio and Girolamo, and Girolamo's son, Nicolò, searched for the perfect balance between volume and expressive sound by experimenting with shapes and sizes. Nicolò Amati's 'Grand Pattern', the best known of the bigger instruments from Cremona, produces some of the most beautiful sounds ever made by a violin. The sweeping curve of his backs and fronts, however, reduces the vibrating area and thus restricts the fullness of tone that later violinists, in particular, demanded from their instruments. Antonio Stradivari, who was probably Nicolò's pupil, experimented after Nicolò's death with a longer soundbox before developing his classic model, shortly after 1700, with a more conventional body length, slightly wider than before, and flatter on the top and back. Stradivari also reduced the depth of the curve along the edge and closed the gap between the purfling and the point at which the arching begins to rise. This provides a balance of sound quality and volume, which ensured, in due course, that his instruments became favoured above all others.

Stradivari was famous in his own lifetime and after, but in the eighteenth century the violins made by Jacob Stainer in Austria were often preferred by soloists and imitated more commonly by makers. The instruments of Stainer and the Amatis, however, could not cope as well as those of Stradivari with the range of effects required by nineteenth-century violinists and composers, and, because of this, the Stradivari violin emerged early in the century as the preferred pattern.

The greater tonal power and brilliance demanded from the violin by much late eighteenth- and early nineteenth-century music brought about a number of final adjustments in the structure of the neck and soundbox. These changes had drastic consequences for earlier instruments that were almost universally rebuilt to match the new requirements. Increased tension on the strings led to the insertion of a larger bass bar and thicker soundpost. The bridge was heightened and the neck was extended to carry a longer length of string. In many cases the neck length was altered by removing the neck altogether and inserting a longer one, but the same result could be achieved, less drastically, by inserting a block of wood between the neck and the soundbox. Necks were originally attached almost parallel to the ribs, but the higher bridge of the nineteenth-century violin required a more tilted neck, and, because of this, the inserted wood is wedge-shaped and the neck joins the body at an angle. These changes were made because ancient violins were then valued, as they still are, by players, often in preference to modern instruments.

Lira da braccio by Giovanni Maria of Brescia (working c.1560–c.1590)

Printed label: *Gioanmaria bresiano / in Venezia*

Length with neck: 647; length of body: 387; width of upper, middle, and lower bouts: 187, 135, 234; max. depth of sides: 34; string length: 323

Boyden, no. 8
Presented by W. E. Hill & Sons, 1939

The lira da braccio, a bowed instrument played under the chin or against the chest like the violin, is familiar in sixteenth-century Italian art. The Ashmolean lira, however, is one of the few instruments of this kind that survives. The pegbox, ebony fingerboard, and tailpiece appear to be original. The instrument shows little sign of wear, especially on the pegbox, where the gold mauresque pattern is as fresh as when it was painted. Unlike the violin, which had three or four strings, this lira has seven strings, two of which are sympathetic strings mounted alongside the fingerboard. Instruments of this type with a distinctive leaf-shaped pegbox and frontally inserted pegs are known from the early 1500s and throughout the century. The belief, at one time, that the maker of this instrument was born in the mid-fifteenth century encouraged the idea that it was extremely early. According to David Boyden, however, the label is printed in a type not used earlier than 1570. As Boyden also points out, the mauresque ornament in the pegbox cannot date from before 1520 at the earliest. These problems, which troubled Boyden, were solved by the musicologist Laurence Witten, who attributed both this instrument and the Ashmolean's treble viol (see p. 4) to a Giovanni Maria who worked in Venice at the end of the sixteenth century. A slightly larger but similar instrument appears in Titian's *The Flaying of Marsyas* (Kromeriz Archiepiscopal Palace), dating from the early 1570s. It has been suggested that the Ashmolean lira is identical with an instrument that once belonged to the Hungarian collector Alexander

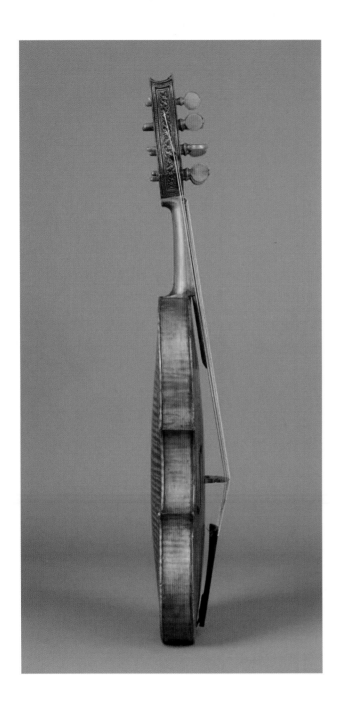

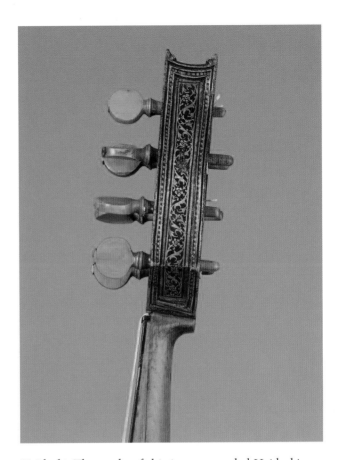

Hajdecki. The study of this instrument led Hajdecki to form his widely accepted theory of the link between the lira and the evolution of the violin. His lira, however, had a label with the name of Gaspard Tieffenbrucker, dated 1515. If these are the same instruments, the label of Giovanni Maria must have been inserted between 1892 (the date of Hajdecki's book) and 1904, when the Ashmolean lira was exhibited in London. But, with a better knowledge of the documents, the label no longer seems as doubtful as it did. Hajdecki's instrument was probably another of the same type, almost certainly with a fake label, and dated too early.

Viola by Gasparo da Salò (1540–1609)

Printed label: *Gasparo da Salò in Brescia / 1561* (the date added in ink)

Length with neck: 655; length of body: 420; width of upper, middle, and lower bouts: 213, 158, 258; max. depth: 38; string length: 353

Boyden, no. 9
Presented by W. E. Hill & Sons, 1939

This is essentially a viola with features that are typical of the lira da braccio. The single corners, marking the beginning of the lower bouts, are commonly found on sixteenth-century lire da braccio, but the f-holes, pegbox, scroll, and maple ribs with overhanging back and front, both arching outwards, are also characteristic of the violin family. In particular, it has four strings, tuned like the modern viola. The two-piece back and ribs are made of maple, and the front is made of spruce, cut to show a grain pattern similar to the grain on the fronts of Gasparo's bass viol and cittern in the Ashmolean. The short neck, fingerboard, and tailpiece are not original but have been restored in the old style. The pegbox and scroll, grafted onto the neck, likewise are of authentic design but may not be original. The broad, upright f-holes with eyes of equal size are typically Brescian. This apparently hybrid form might suggest that the instrument was made by Gasparo not long after his arrival in Brescia. He is generally supposed to have arrived in about 1562, but, if the date written in pen and ink on the label is to be believed, he must have been already in the city in 1561. Gasparo's labels, however, are very rarely dated, and this date was surely added later. If the pegbox is (as it seems) a skilful imitation of an original viola pegbox, it is likely that this was once a true lira da braccio, adapted as a viola when the lira da braccio passed out of fashion; in this case there is no need to suppose it was made as early as the 1560s. It belonged, at one time, to the family of the Dukes of Este in Modena.

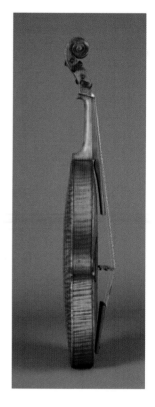

Violin by Andrea Amati (c.1505–77)

Label, written in red ink: *AND [...] / C [...] ONA MDLXIV*

Length with neck: 574; length of body: 342; width of upper, middle, and lower bouts: 159, 107, 196; max. depth of sides: 29; string length: 317

Topham, 1487
Boyden, no. 10
Presented by W. E. Hill & Sons, 1939

This small violin, made in 1564, is the earliest known dated violin. The motto on the ribs: PIETATE ET IUSTITIA ('by piety and justice') and the emblems painted on the back, now badly worn, identify it as one of a set of instruments commissioned from Andrea Amati of Cremona for the court of the French king, Charles IX (1550–74). This set is first mentioned, briefly, by Jean-Benjamin de Laborde in his history of music published in 1780, and again in 1806 by the abbé Sibire, who described the painted decoration in detail. It is said that these instruments were removed from Versailles during the Revolution and dispersed. This violin, however, had left the royal collection much earlier, as it is branded twice on the lower ribs and again on the scroll with the initials of the violinist and composer William Corbett (1668–1748), who bequeathed his collection of instruments, including several by the Amatis, to Gresham College. They were subsequently sold. The violin is next recorded in the collection of General Zelaziewitch, who lived in Ryde on the Isle of Wight. It was bought at his auction by Major Henry J. Way. He showed it to the Hills in 1894, and they bought it ten years later. The commissioning of these instruments by the French court acknowledged Amati's reputation as one of the foremost makers of stringed instruments in Italy. At present, only ten of the instruments from this group have been identified: four small violins, one large violin, one tenor viola (also in the Ashmolean), and four cellos, although other decorated instruments of this type by Andrea Amati are known. Several variations in the painted designs and other minor differences between the instruments suggest that they were probably commissioned at various periods during the king's brief reign and, on each occasion, painted slightly differently from a pattern sent to Cremona from France. The two instruments in the Ashmolean belong to a distinct group within the larger set that includes an almost identical violin, now in Tullie House in Carlisle, and another in the museum in Cremona. The Ashmolean violin is of exquisite craftsmanship. The front and back are edged with a neat single line of purfling, drawn to a sharp point in the corners, and the f-holes of a typical Amati form are cut fairly broad with large upper eyes. The one-piece back and the ribs are made of maple. The scroll is original, but the neck, fingerboard, pegs, and tailpiece are later. There are many signs of wear, but it is generally well preserved.

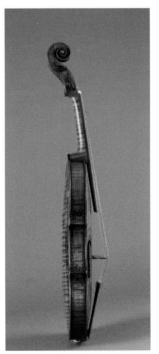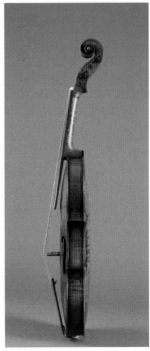

Viola by Andrea Amati (c.1505–77)

Label, inscribed in black: *ANDREA AMADI IN / CREMONA M.D.LXXI-IIj*

Length with neck: 750; length of body: 470; width of upper, middle, and lower bouts: 229, 157, 270; max. depth of sides: 40; string length: 403

Topham, 1500
Boyden, no. 11
Presented by W. E. Hill & Sons, 1939

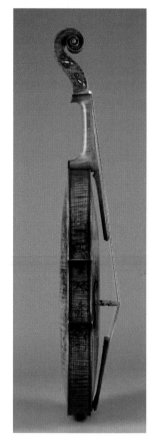

Like the Andrea Amati violin, this sumptuous viola came from the set of instruments made for the French court during the reign of Charles IX. The violin was made near the beginning of his reign, whereas the viola label is dated 1573, a year before the king's death. The label, however, appears to be a photocopy of a genuine label from another instrument and cannot be taken as evidence that the viola dates from so many years after its companion. It is a large instrument, which has fortunately escaped the reduction in size inflicted on other large violas from this early period. The tailpiece is old and probably original; it has a little silver plate fitted over the gut, possibly added much later to protect the gut from damage. The fingerboard is not original but has been inlaid to match the tailpiece. The neck, also, is not old, but the pegbox and scroll are original. Like all the known instruments from this set, it is inscribed along the ribs with the king's motto, PIETATE ET IUSTITIA, and the back is decorated with allegorical figures of Piety and Justice, letters K (for 'Karolus'), crowned columns, putti with crowns, the chain and badge of the order of Saint-Michel, and three fleurs-de-lys. The back is made of two-piece maple. The spruce front is varnished golden brown and neatly inlaid with a line of purfling. Topham's date for both instruments from the Charles IX set (1500 for the viola, 1487 for the violin) suggests a long period of seasoning and also provides evidence that, despite some doubt that has been expressed about the age of these instruments, both are, in fact, as old as the emblems and inscription suggest. Comparison with the front of the Charles IX violin in Cremona indicates that both instruments were made from wood from the same tree. The Hills bought this viola between 1920 and 1925 from the maker and restorer Josef Vedral in The Hague. According to the Hill archives, it was in the collection of a count in Warsaw in the first half of the nineteenth century. Paganini saw it there during a concert tour. Subsequently, it was acquired by a Schubert family in St Petersburg, from where it passed, after the Revolution, to Finland and hence to Vedral, who bought it from a naval lieutenant.

Viola by Gasparo da Salò
(1540–1609)

This viola, like the Andrea Amati viola, has escaped the fate of other early large violas, which have been cut down to the modern size. The ribs are battered, particularly where they join the neck. The pegbox has been snapped in half, but has been skilfully repaired by the insertion of thin plates of carefully matched wood on both cheeks. Nevertheless, it is remarkably intact. The fingerboard with an inlaid lozenge pattern, the matching tailpiece with two ivory buttons, the pegbox and scroll all seem to be original. Only the bridge, pegs, and the ivory nut are not old. The elegant swell on front and back, the chunky scroll, and the long, upright f-holes with eyes of almost equal size on top and bottom are typically Brescian.

Printed label: *Gasparo da Salò. In Brescia.*

Length with neck: 697; length of body: 444; width of upper, middle, and lower bouts: 444, 218, 147; max. depth of sides: 38; string length: 368

Topham, 1533
Boyden, no. 12
Presented by W. E. Hill & Sons, 1939

Viola by the brothers Amati: Antonio (c.1540–1607) and Girolamo (c.1561–1630)

This viola is branded with the letter M on the button, like the museum's bass viol of 1611, and with a crowned orb or letter O. On the evidence of an Amati viola, dated 1595, branded with a similar orb and decorated with the arms of the Medici, the musicologist Laurence Witten has suggested, tentatively, that these instruments may have been commissioned by the Medici in Florence. There is a viola in a private collection – formerly in the collection of Lord Wilton – attributed to Andrea Amati, which is branded on the scroll with the same mark, suggesting that the brand belonged to someone who owned or commissioned a group of instruments by the Amatis. The front of this viola is made of spruce, finely grained on the sides with more open grain in the arching. The ribs and two-piece back are made of maple with a square of purfling at the base where the ivory end-pin is set inside a purfled diamond. The purfling at the base, as John Dilworth has pointed out, may not be original. The fingerboard is a replacement, inlaid to match the tailpiece, which is original. The neck has been reworked with an inserted wooden plug at the button and a reduction at the heel, which has exposed the nail holes, where the neck was originally secured to the upper block. This viola once belonged to Sir William Hamilton (1730–1803), British plenipotentiary at Naples from 1764 to 1800.

Printed label: *Anton [...] & Hieronymus Fr. Amati / Cremonen Andreae fil. F. 1592* (the date added in pen and ink)

Length with neck: 725; length of body: 454; width of upper, middle, and lower bouts: 220, 152, 266; max. depth of sides: 40; string length: 394
Topham, 1533

Boyden, no. 13
Presented by W. E. Hill & Sons, 1939

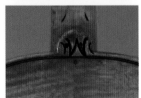

Violin by the brothers Amati: Antonio (*c.*1540–1607) and Girolamo (*c.*1561–1630)

This little violin, only 555 mm from scroll to end-pin, is a perfect example of the work of Girolamo Amati, with a finely patterned two-piece back of maple. The neck is not original, but the scroll, grafted below the nut, is in the typical Amati style, pinched at the top and boldly cut. The fluting at the back of the scroll is worn from sliding the instrument into its original case, and the corners are a little blunted with use. The inlaid ebony fingerboard and tailpiece are modern. David Boyden suggests that it may have been designed for a child.

Printed label: *Antonius & Hieronymus Fr. Amati / Cremonen Andreae fil. F. 1618* (the date added in ink)

Length with neck: 555; length of body: 331; width of upper, middle, and lower bouts: 153, 104, 189; max. depth of sides: 27; string length: 310
Boyden, no. 14
Presented by A. Phillips Hill in accordance with the wishes of Alfred and Arthur Hill, 1948

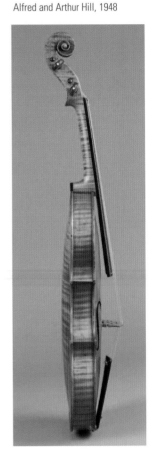

Violin ('The Alard') by Nicolò Amati (1596–1684)

Printed label: *Nicolaus Amatus Cremonen. Hieronymi / Fil. ac Antonij Nepos Fecit. 1649* (the last two digits of the date added in ink)

Length with neck: 583; length of body: 351; width of upper, middle, and lower bouts: 163, 111, 203; max. depth of sides: 29; string length: 328

Boyden, no. 15
Presented by A. Phillips Hill in accordance with the wishes of Arthur and Alfred Hill, 1948

Nicolò Amati, as his label indicates, was the son of Girolamo and nephew of Antonio. He continued the great tradition of his family, making instruments of unprecedented splendour and musical quality, which set a standard for future makers. Stradivari is said to have been one of his many pupils. This shapely instrument, as curvaceous as a Baroque church, is one of the finest in the Hill Collection. There is much wear, but it is wonderfully intact. The neck is original, although it has been lengthened, and old nail holes have been exposed where the thickness of the heel has been reduced. The two-piece back and ribs are made from finely patterned maple, coloured nut brown. The ribs at the base are made of one continuous strip of wood. The f-holes are particularly elegant, cut narrow towards the ends, with broad wings and small upper eyes. In the late nineteenth century, this violin belonged to the famous violinist Delphin Alard, who also owned 'The Messiah'.

Violin by Jacob Stainer (1617?–83)

Label, handwritten in ink, faded and partly obscured with an ink blot over the maker's name: *[…] er in Absam / prope […] Fecit [?] 1672*

Length with neck: 585; length of body: 353; width of upper, middle, and lower bouts: 167, 110, 206; max. depth of sides: 30; string length: 323

Topham, 1547
Boyden, no. 16
Bequeathed by the Revd E. C. Tippetts, 1957

Jacob Stainer, who worked in Absam in the Austrian Tyrol, at one time enjoyed a reputation greater than that of Nicolò Amati and Stradivari. The steep arching of his instruments encouraged the idea that he had been a pupil of Nicolò. While there is no documentary evidence to suggest that he had trained with Nicolò, there exists one label by Stainer that states that the instrument had been made in Cremona. If this inscription can be trusted, it suggests that he would, at least, have been familiar with Nicolò's work. The f-holes of this violin are particularly upright. The neat purfling is taken sharply into the corners, finished at the point with pen and ink. The pegbox and scroll are probably original, but the neck is not. The ebony fingerboard and 'duck-bill' tailpiece are also new. The back is made from one piece of maple, extended on both sides, in the lower bouts, with added strips of maple. The label is almost illegible but, as David Boyden points out, should read: *Jacobus Stainer in Absam / prope Oenipontum Fecit 1672* – that is, 'Jacob Stainer made this in Absam near Innsbruck, 1672'.

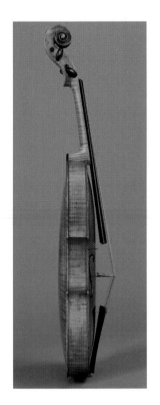

Violin by Francesco Rugeri (c.1630–98)

Printed label: *Francesco Regeri ditto II Per / in Cremona 1696* (the last digit added in ink)

Length with neck: 586; length of body: 354; width of upper, middle, and lower bouts: 167, 111, 205; max. depth of sides: 36; string length: 330

Acc. no: WA1992.297
Bequeathed by Alfred Frederick Hird, 1992.

Rugeri worked in Cremona and is said to have been a pupil of Nicolò Amati, but there is no evidence of this other than the fact that he imitated Nicolò's style with flair. This violin is based on an Amati model with a swelling front and shapely back. The neck is not original, but has been grafted onto the pegbox along the lower cheeks, cutting through the first peghole. The thin purfling on the pine front is somewhat blurred, and the f-holes are noticeably asymmetrical. The back and sides are made of maple. Rugeri's labels are inscribed with his name in a variety of forms. Most date from the 1670s and 1680s.

Violin by Antonio Stradivari (1644?–1737)

Printed label: *Antonius Stradivarius Cremonensis / Faciebat Anno 1683* (the last digit added in ink)

Length with neck: 575; length of body: 340; width of upper, middle, and lower bouts: 153, 107, 192; max. depth of sides: 32; string length: 318

Boyden, no. 17
Presented by W. E. Hill & Sons, 1946

The similarities between instruments made by Stradivari from 1667 to the mid-1680s and those made by Nicolò Amati have encouraged the belief that Stradivari was a pupil of Amati. This small violin was made towards the end of this first period and still follows the Amati model. It is unusually ornate. The purfling is inlaid with little ivory lozenges, separated by ivory circles, there is an eight-pointed star of mother-of-pearl in the button, and the scroll is inlaid with a tendril ornament, completed with a little paint. A similar design, cut into the wood and filled with black mastic, runs along the ribs in short, scrolling sections. A paper pattern for the decoration on the scroll and similar patterns for rib designs survive in the Stradivari museum in Cremona. The front is spruce, the back and sides are maple. The ebony fingerboard and tailpiece, inlaid in the same style, are not old, but the neck is original, with two later separate insertions between the neck and upper block. The nail holes, exposed when the heel was recut, have been plugged. Only ten other decorated instruments of this type by Stradivari are known: five in the Smithsonian Institution in Washington, four in the royal palace in Madrid, and one in a private collection. They were all surely intended for important clients. The Ashmolean violin belonged at one time to the Este family, who may have commissioned it. It was bought from the Este by Cipriani Potter, from whom it passed to the Hills in the late nineteenth century.

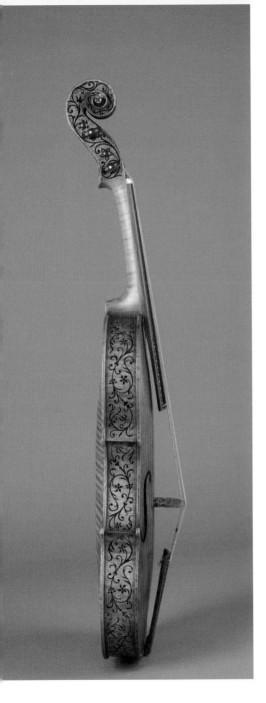
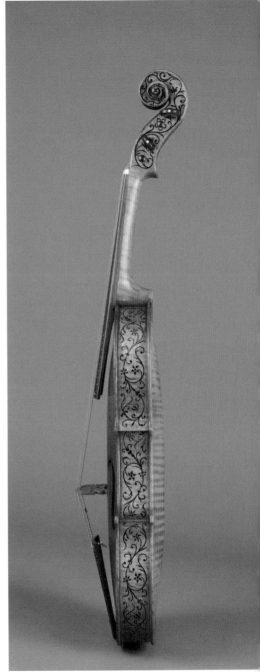

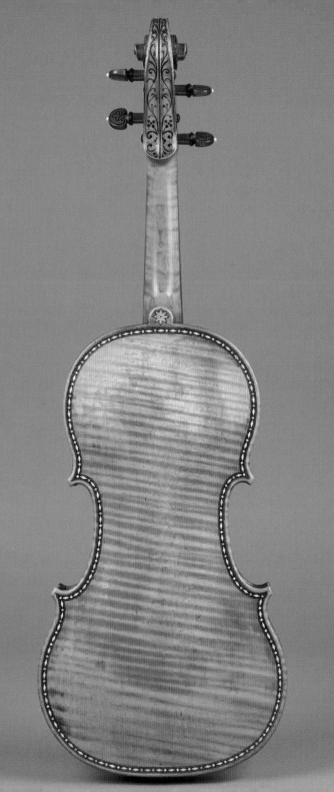

Violin ('The Messiah') by Antonio Stradivari (1644?–1737)

Printed label: *Antonius Stradivarius, Cremonensis / Faciebat Anno 1716* (the last digit added in ink)

Length with neck: 593; length of body: 356; width of upper, middle, and lower bouts: 168, 112, 213; max. depth of sides: 32; string length: 330

Topham, 1682
Boyden, no. 18
Presented by W. E. Hill & Sons, 1940

'The Messiah' dates from Stradivari's 'Golden Period', the years from 1700 to 1718 when he was at the height of his powers, making instruments on a pattern that has been imitated ever since. 'The Messiah' has not survived unaltered, but the lack of wear and the fresh appearance of the varnish set it apart from any other violin by Stradivari and from most by any ancient maker. It owes its remarkable state of preservation to the fact that, throughout its history, it has been a 'collector's piece', rarely played and carefully protected by successive owners. It has been linked to a violin of 1716 in untouched condition mentioned in the notes of the Milanese collector Cozio di Salabue, which Salabue bought from Stradivari's youngest son in 1775. Despite references to a patch inside Salabue's violin that is not now visible inside 'The Messiah', it is likely that this was the instrument that Salabue sold to the dealer Luigi Tarisio in 1827. The details of the sale to Tarisio were written on the upper plate inside the violin by Jean-Baptiste Vuillaume, the famous French maker, who bought it from Tarisio's heirs in 1855. Tarisio had often boasted to his friends in Paris that he had a violin by Stradivari in exceptional condition, provoking the violinist Delphin Alard to say: 'Your violin is like The Messiah. It is always expected but never appears.' Hence, apparently, its present name. It was probably Tarisio, himself, who first jokingly referred to it as 'The Messiah' in conversation with Vuillaume and his colleagues. Vuillaume, with good reason, assumed that this was the violin in question when he found it in 1855 in

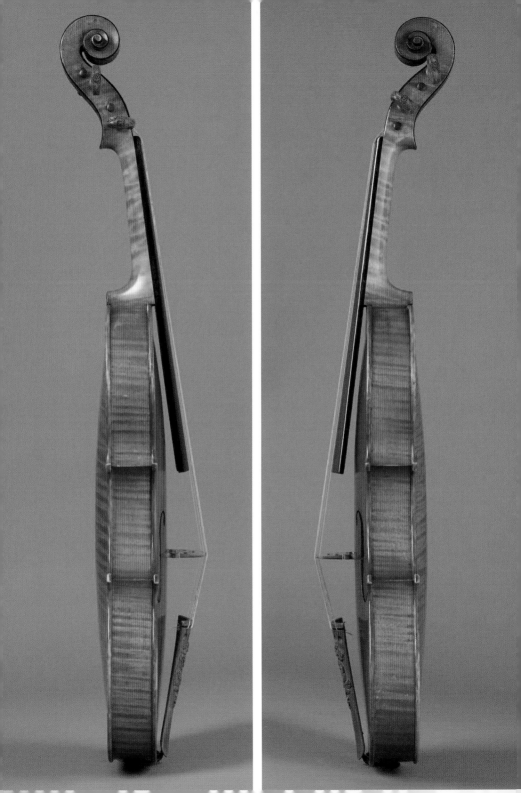

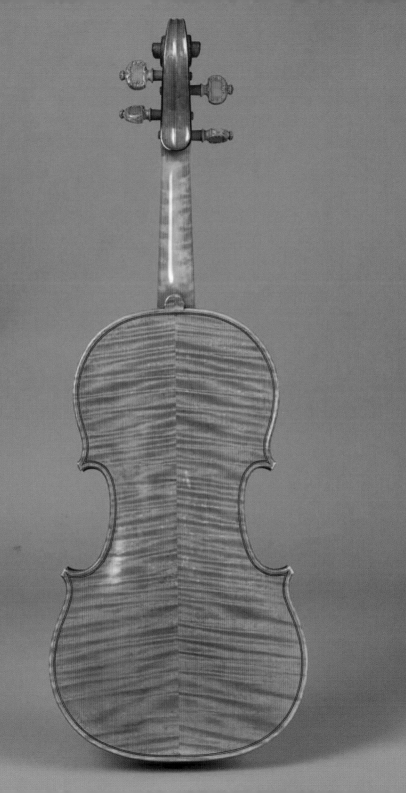

a farmhouse belonging to Tarisio's family. So did the English novelist Charles Reade, who knew Tarisio and had also heard the story of the elusive violin. This history explains why it shows so little sign of wear. With the exception of Vuillaume's son-in-law, Delphin Alard, none of those who have owned 'The Messiah' has been a professional player. It is not, however, as pristine as it appears. Vuillaume lengthened the neck, inserting a visible wedge between the heel and body, and fitted it with a new sound bar, pegs, fingerboard, and a carved boxwood tailpiece representing the Nativity of Christ in an allusion to the name by which it is popularly known. He made these changes to make it playable. Since the time when it was altered by Vuillaume, it has been played in private by Joachim, Piatti, Aldo Simonetti, Nathan Milstein, surely by Alard, and by others. But these were rare exceptions in the history of a violin that has been carefully protected by its owners for the past three centuries from the rigours of excessive handling.

Recent scrutiny of 'The Messiah' has added a wealth of unexpected information about the history of the instrument. The discovery that the sprucewood front closely matches the wood of two instruments by Stradivari of 1717 – one so closely that it is probably from the same tree – confirms the date inscribed upon the label. In 1997 a previously unnoticed form mark, a letter G, written in pen and ink, was found inside the pegbox. Letters like this were probably once common in Stradivari's pegboxes, but would have been removed when the necks and the ends of the pegboxes were cut out in the nineteenth century. These letters correspond to numbers on Stradivari's wooden templates that survive in Cremona along with his tools and many of his paper patterns. 'The Messiah', however, corresponds not to the G form but to the fractionally smaller PG form, round which its outline fits neatly. Was this a mistake in the workshop? Or were the two forms so close it did not matter which pegbox was used? There may be a clue to this in the tiny seven-pointed star that has been impressed twice on either side of the G mark in the pegbox and once in the centre of the scroll eye on the treble side. Stars are found impressed on several of the wooden templates in Cremona, but these are of a different type and their purpose has not yet been convincingly explained. The survival of these details and the fresh appearance of the instrument are what make it so remarkable today, but there is nothing to suggest that, when it was new, it was any different from other violins by Stradivari dating from his 'Golden Period'. There is a slight asymmetry in the placing of the f-holes, a touch of carelessness that is found in a number of his violins, and the scroll eyes are not perfectly balanced. Stradivari was a wonderful craftsman, but he designed his instruments to make music, and, unlike modern makers, he was not obsessed by the need to achieve perfection in details where it did not matter.

Violin with the label of Edward Pamphilon (*c.*1646–after 1685)

Handwritten label: *Edward Pamphilon / Anno 1669*

Length with neck: 590; length of body: 348; width of upper, middle, and lower bouts: 169, 113, 202; max. depth of sides: 39; string length: 323

Topham, 1697
Cooper, ii. 130–5
Acc. no: WA1999.26
Presented by Albert Cooper, 1999

Edward Pamphilon is the best-known member of a family of violin-makers based in Essex in the seventeenth and eighteenth centuries. Sandys and Forster mention a tradition that he traded from a shop on London Bridge in partnership with Thomas Urquhart, who is said to have been his master. The Hills noted a close similarity between Pamphilon's violins and those by Urquhart, but little is known about his life, and there is no sound evidence about his training. His workshop has not been identified, but the fact that his instruments appear to have been sold by John Miller on London Bridge might account for the belief that his workshop was there. The scroll on this violin is vigorously cut and rather coarse in appearance, with evident chisel marks where the flutes end at the top of the pegbox; the eyes are prominent but the second turn of the scroll is distinctly flat. The neck is a replacement. The back is made of two-piece figured maple. The front is steeply arched with widely cut f-holes ending in narrow wings. The setting of the ribs into a groove along the back is a feature associated with Pamphilon's work. However, the discrepancy between the date on the label and the results of the tree-ring dating is troublesome, casting doubt on the reliability of the label (which is suspiciously fresh) and suggesting that the violin might have been made by a maker in Pamphilon's circle, perhaps by another member of his family.

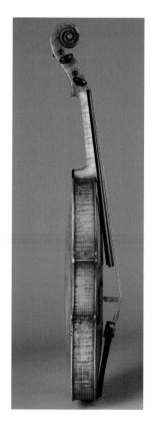

Viola with the label of Peter Wamsley (*c.*1670–1744)

Printed label: *Made by Peter Wamsley / at ye Golden Harp in Pickadilly*

Length with neck: 670; length of body: 410; width of upper, middle, and lower bouts: 194, 143, 235; max. depth of sides: 44; string length: 381

Topham, 1746
Cooper, ii. 190–5
Acc. no: WA1999.23
Presented by Albert Cooper, 1999

Wamsley was trading at his shop The Golden Harp (later changed to The Harp and Hautboy) by the mid-1720s. After his death in 1744, his obituary in the *Daily Advertiser* noted that 'he was reckoned by most good judges to be the best maker of violins and violincellos that ever was in England'. The back of this viola is made from one piece of lightly striated maple, rising steeply from the sides and flattening in the centre. The front, made from close-grained softwood, is similarly arched with distinct hollows along the edges, somewhat in the manner of Jacob Stainer. The bottom ribs are made from a single strip of maple. The button is lop-sided and may have been recut when a new neck was inserted at an angle to the body. The pegbox is original, but the ebony pegs, fingerboard, and 'duck-bill' tailpiece are modern. This is a fine instrument in Wamsley's manner, but violas by him are not common, and the result of the tree-ring analysis suggests that it could have been made by his pupil Thomas Smith, who took over Wamsley's business in 1751. Among Wamsley's other pupils was Joseph Hill, the first of the Hill dynasty.

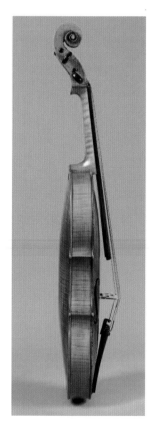

Violin by Nicolas Lupot (1758–1824)

Nicolas Lupot was the most famous member of a family of French instrument-makers, originating in the seventeenth century. He is known as the 'French Stradivari' partly because he produced instruments of outstanding quality and partly because he took Stradivari's instruments as his model. This handsome violin has the wide, flattish arching of the classic Stradivari, but the fine, transparent, orange-red varnish is Lupot's own. The neck is new, but the pegbox is original. The maple back is richly ornamented with the orders of Saint-Michel and the Saint-Esprit and other emblems of the French royal family. The inscription on the ribs records the award of this instrument to a student at the Royal School of Music in Paris in 1818. In 1816 Lupot became maker to the Royal School and, in this capacity, supplied an annual prize instrument to the best pupil. The winner of this violin has been identified as Joseph Clavel, a pupil of Rodolphe Kreutzer, who became a violinist at the Théatre Italien. Lupot was aware of the instruments made by Andrea Amati for Charles IX – he repaired at least one – and probably had these in mind when decorating this violin.

Printed label: *Nicolas Lupot, Lauthier, rue Croix / des petits-Champs, à Paris, l'an 1816* (the date added in ink). There is a brand at the top of the inside back: *N Lupot / à Paris* below an eagle and dated 1815 in ink. A label from Wurlitzer's 1925 catalogue is also gummed to the back inside.

Length with neck: 590; length of body: 357; width of upper, middle, and lower bouts: 168, 120, 209; max. depth of sides: 39; string length: 330

Topham, 1794
Cooper, ii. 124–9, 196–9
Acc. no: WA1999.24
Presented by Albert Cooper, 1999

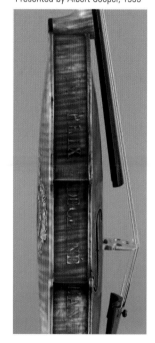

 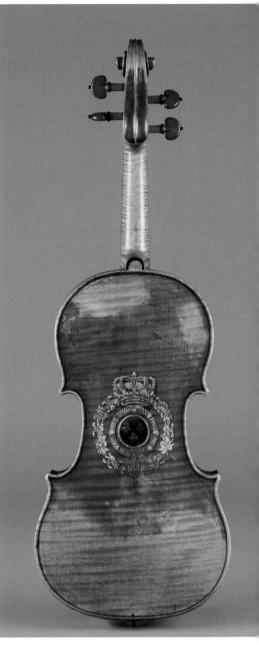

Viola by Simon Andrew Forster (1801–70)

Printed label: *S. A. Forster / London*. Inscribed in ink on the lower ribs below the tailpin: *S. A. Forster / London / no. 7*

Length with neck: 690; length of body: 420; width of upper, middle, and lower bouts: 197, 142, 247; max. depth of sides: 49; string length: 371

Topham, 1745
Cooper, ii. 88–93
Acc. no: WA1999.25
Presented by Albert Cooper, 1999

Simon Forster belonged to the fourth generation of a family of instrument-makers based in London. From the mid-1820s, he made instruments of two classes, one of a high quality and the other of lesser quality with a cheaper alcohol-based varnish. This large viola is an instrument of the first class, one of eleven numbered violas made by Forster between 1839 and 1843. The key to his numbering system, which he published in the *History of the Violin* (1864), written in collaboration with his solicitor, William Sandys, dates the Ashmolean viola to 1843. Forster also noted that it was unsold at the time of writing. The neck was made to the modern standard and has not been altered. The rich transparent red varnish, covering the spruce front and maple back, is well preserved, but repaired pegholes suggest that the instrument has been played extensively.

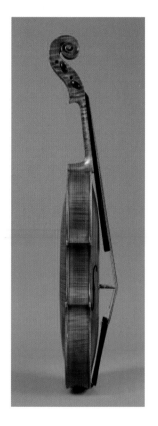

Kit violin (mid-eighteenth century)

Length with neck: 460; length of body: 185; width of upper, middle, and lower bouts: 85, 62, 100; max. depth of sides: 28; string length: 300

Acc. no: WA1999.27
Presented by Albert Cooper, 1999

A kit is a type of small, portable violin used by dancing masters and itinerant musicians from the sixteenth to the nineteenth century. It exists in a narrow stick shape that could be carried in a tubular case, or in the form of a miniature viol or violin with a long neck. This kit is shaped like a little viol with sloping shoulders. It has a diamond-shaped design of purfling on the back. The front of one-piece spruce and back of one-piece maple are steeply arched. The f-holes are short and set low. Despite a repaired break below the button, it is in good condition, preserving its original maple neck and peg-box and, perhaps, its original pegs. It has been attributed to a follower or contemporary of Henry Jaye (working c.1740–76), who specialized in making kit violins in mid-eighteenth-century London.

Length with neck: 475; length of
body: 217; width of upper, middle,
and lower bouts: 111, 77, 127;
max. depth of sides: 29; string
length: 297

Cooper, ii. 8–9
Acc. no: WA1999.28
Presented by Albert Cooper, 1999

Kit violin (eighteenth century)

This kit violin is also shaped like a viol. The ribs and
one-piece back are made of maple. The back of the scroll
is built up with an added section that has been repaired
by the insertion of a slip of wood along the upper join.
Both of the lower ribs have been extended by small
inserts, nailed to the corner blocks. Kit violins went out
of fashion in the early nineteenth century, but this one
must have remained in long use, as the neck has been
tilted to the nineteenth-century standard by the insertion of a new heel. There is an inscription, written in
pen and ink on the inside of the front: *H Robinson /
Wilson Street / 1821*, probably put there by the
repairer when the neck was altered.

3. Citterns

The cittern was a wire-strung instrument played with a plectrum. It appears to have evolved in the fifteenth century from the medieval citole, a small plucked instrument familiar in illuminated manuscripts from the thirteenth century onwards but possibly much older. In the earliest citterns, the body, neck, and pegbox are carved from one block of hardwood with a separate front and fingerboard. Citterns like the three in the Ashmolean are of a more refined type that developed in Italy in the last decades of the sixteenth century. These have a pear-shaped front, like the earlier citterns, pierced by an inset rose, but the back and sides are made from separate pieces of wood and the fingerboard projects over the soundbox. The body is shallow and wedge-shaped when looked at from the side, tapering towards the lower end. The neck is fretted with metal bars and has a channel along the back on the bass side to allow the player's left thumb to slide easily up and down. The peghead is inclined slightly backwards and the pegs are inserted frontally, carrying wire strings originally gathered in six courses, either double courses or single and double courses combined, which pass over a low bridge and are fixed to pins on the bottom. The top four courses of the Italian cittern were normally tuned a, g, d, e, with some variation in the tuning of the other two. At the point where the neck joins the sides, there are small rolls, called wings, which have no obvious use but may have been added to reinforce a supposed similarity with the ancient Greek *kithara* from which the words *cittern* and *guitar* derive. Many are fitted with a hook on the back of the neck by which it could be suspended when not in use.

The cittern had a widespread appeal, rivalling the lute, which is a more complex and cumbersome instrument. It was associated with inns and barbers' shops, but it was also played by wealthy amateurs, and much fine music was written for it. It was equally popular in northern Europe in a four-course variant with lateral pegs and some difference in the tuning. By the middle of the seventeenth century, the fashion began to slip, and many citterns were restrung as a form of popular guitar. No doubt the rise of the guitar was in part responsible for the demise of the cittern.

Cittern by Gasparo da Salò (1540–1609)

printed label: *Gasparo da Salò In Brescia:* branded on the button: *GASPAR DE SALLO IN BRESA*

length with neck: 743; length of body: 353; width: 222; max. depth of sides: 45; string length: 453

Boyden, no. 31
Presented by W. E. Hill & Sons, 1939

This engaging instrument is a typical late sixteenth-century Brescian cittern. It is branded on the button with the maker's name enclosing a marine creature, perhaps a siren, the mythical Greek creature with a seductive singing voice. The dialect form of the inscription has been taken as evidence of an early date in Gasparo's Brescian career. The branding iron, however, may have been made much earlier than the instrument itself: in any case, the paper label conforms to Gasparo's standard type. The peghead is fitted with eleven pegs (not original) inserted laterally and attached to wire strings, arranged in four double courses and three single courses. The rose and woman's head, carved on the top of the peghead, are gilt. There is a wooden hook at the back, carved, as is usual, in one piece with the neck. The spruce front, cut to show a lattice pattern in the grain, is decorated with double purfling. The back is made of undecorated maple, coloured a rich, deep reddish brown. The sides, head, and neck are also made of maple.

Cittern, attributed to Girolamo Virchi (*c.*1532–after 1574)

length with neck: 800; length of body: 370; width: 234; max. depth of sides: 45; string length: 465.

Topham, 1487
Boyden, no. 33
Presented by W. E. Hill & Sons, 1939

The back of this ornate instrument has been fitted neatly within the sides, a relic, perhaps, of the construction of the earlier sixteenth-century cittern where the back and sides were carved from a single block. The shallow sides and back, carved in low relief in the form of a scallop shell, are made of maple. The front, glued down onto the sides without an overhang, is made of yellow larch. The elaborate carved ornament includes a satyr and satyress on the hook, a relief of Adam and Eve in the Garden of Eden on the button, and a woman's head on top of the pegbox, rising from the mouth of a monster with ram's horns and eyes of black glass. The woman's eyes are inset with red beads. A blue stone, perhaps a turquoise, is set into the top of her head; a diamond-shaped stone was once suspended from a chain around her neck, while holes, pierced through her ears, were perhaps made for ear-rings or suspended pearls. Other coloured beads or gems are set into the back of the pegbox. Double lines of purfling flow from the front onto the sides and form a looping shell-like pattern on the back, wobbling slightly in the tighter bends. Twelve pegs, inserted frontally, carry strings in six double courses. There are signs of eighteen former pegholes set in three rows in the peghead. Other evidence of the earlier stringing was removed when new strips of ivory were inserted on the bridge and saddle and when the back, where the strings are fixed to pins, was rebuilt. It is, however, most unlikely that the cittern was intended to carry eighteen strings. An extension, running along the right side of the fingerboard, was probably added when the number of

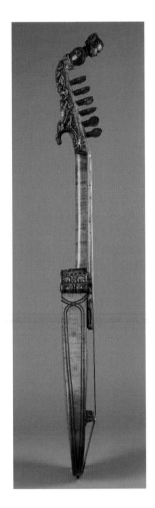

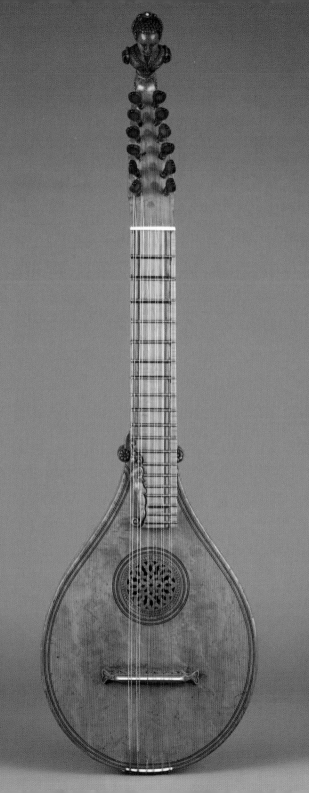

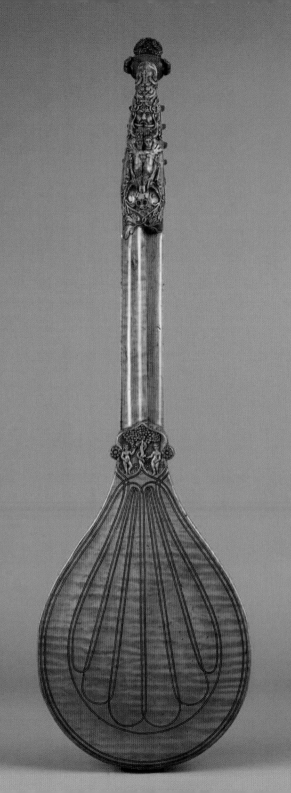

strings was increased. The metal frets, which are of the same width as the present fingerboard, were added then or later. There is a very similar cittern in the Musée de la Musique in Paris, once absurdly attributed to Stradivari, which must have been made in the same workshop. The cittern in Paris has been attributed to Girolamo Virchi of Brescia by comparison with a famous cittern made in 1574 for Archduke Ferdinand of the Tyrol, now in the Kunsthistorisches Museum in Vienna. It is tempting to believe that all three were made by Virchi, but, with so little known about the work of Virchi, this is difficult to prove.

Cittern, early seventeenth century

length with neck: 760; length of body: 369; width: 233; max. depth of sides: 50; string length: 483.

Boyden, no. 32
Presented by A. Phillips Hill in accordance with the wishes of Arthur and Alfred Hill, 1948

Although it lacks the hook commonly found on the back of the neck, this instrument follows the pattern of the typical Italian cittern. It has an elaborate gilt quatrefoil rose, recessed in tiers like the rose commonly found in contemporary guitars. The carved African boy's head, at the top of the pegbox, is painted black, touched with red, and has ivory or bone eyes and teeth. His ears are pierced for ear-rings. The little projecting wings, flanking the base of the neck, are made from two halves of a split baluster, glued over the join between the neck and body. The fingerboard is faced with rectangles of grainy maple, lightly scalloped, between metal frets. The front, somewhat arched, is made of yellow spruce, edged with alternate pieces of ebony and light wood. The body and rose are outlined in pen and black ink, a cheap and easy alternative to inlaid purfling. Nine ebony pegs, inserted laterally, carry five courses of strings, four of which are double. The back and sides are made of golden maple, and a thick band of maple, stained dark brown, runs vertically through the centre of the back. This is an attractive instrument but of more summary manufacture than its distinguished companions in the Ashmolean. The ornament suggests that it was made in the seventeenth century.

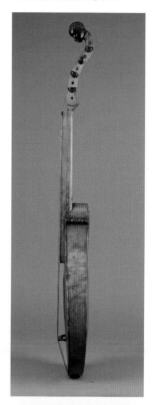

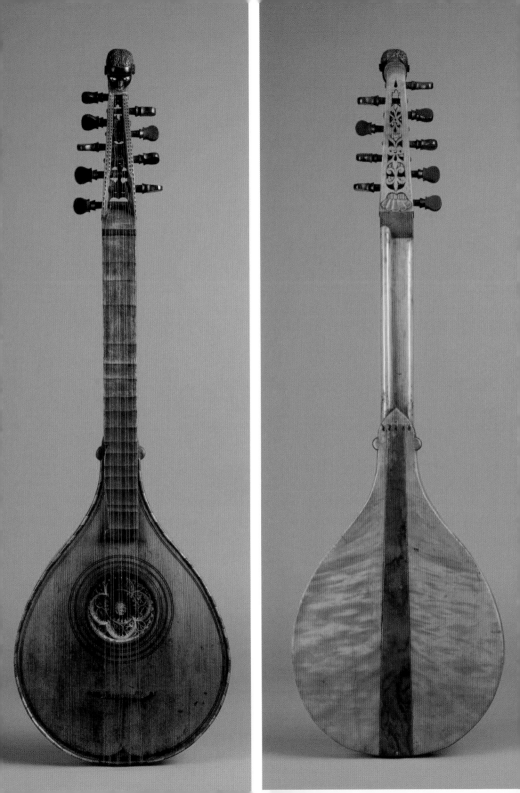

4. Guitars

The guitar derives from the Spanish *vihuela de mano*, the plucked form of the vihuela, a fretted instrument of eleven strings (five double, one single) that was popular in aristocratic society. The guitar seems to have originated in late fifteenth-century Spain as a popular variant of the vihuela with four strings, waisted like the vihuela for ease of playing. By the middle of the sixteenth century, with the addition of a fifth pair of strings and a new tuning – adgbe – the Spanish guitar emerged in the form that lasted more or less until the late eighteenth century. Like the modern guitar, it had a flat back and front and a deep soundbox with incurving sides, but it was a slimmer instrument with a pegbox angled like the head of the lute and was often fretted like the viol with gut cords, marking the semitones. In the early sixteenth century, the Spanish guitar spread quickly through Europe as a rival to the lute, cheaper to make and easier to play. Its use was widespread. Both Charles II of England and Louis XIV of France played the guitar, but it was also popular with itinerant musicians. It is found commonly in middle-class interiors in Dutch seventeenth-century art and it remained in fashion in France and Italy throughout the eighteenth century. It was taken up less enthusiastically in England, where fashionable society in the second half of the eighteenth century preferred the so-called English guitar, an instrument that has more in common with the traditional cittern, although it is bulkier and tuned differently. According to the musicologist Charles Burney, the rage for these 'guittars' undermined the popularity of the harpsichord in English drawing rooms to such an extent that Jacob Kirkman, the eminent maker of harpsichords, bought up a large number of guitars and distributed them to shop girls and street-singers in an attempt to cure society ladies of their 'frivolous and vulgar taste'. When Burney was writing in the early 1800s, the fashion for the English guitar had ended, ousted by the arrival of the Spanish guitar from the Continent. By the 1830s the Spanish guitar had acquired its modern deeply waisted shape, discarded the second row of strings, and acquired an extra string, tuned to e.

Guitar by Giorgio Sellas (first half of the seventeenth century)

inscribed on a mother-of-pearl plaque in the centre of the head:
Giorgio Sellas / alla Stella in / Venetia / 1627 / Fecit.

length with neck: 942; length of body: 445; width of upper, middle, and lower bouts: 210, 192, 255; max. depth of sides: 100; string length: 681.

Topham, 1615
Boyden, no. 39
Presented by W. E. Hill & Sons, 1939

This is a common Italian form of the guitar. Seen from the front, it appears identical to the familiar Spanish guitar, but, unlike the Spanish guitar, it has a deeply rounded back, resembling the lute. Ten pegs, inserted into the back of the head, carry five double courses, which pass through holes in a low bridge and are fixed to five ivory pins at the base. The decoration is particularly rich. The rose-hole, set within a flamboyant pattern of ivory, ebony, and mother-of-pearl inlay, is filled with five elaborately cut layers of gilded parchment or paper. The ornament on the lower front is less well preserved. The wood below the rose is very stained and disfigured by an attempt to conceal cracks on left and right by inserting a pattern of incised tendrils, inlaid with mastic, in imitation of the original design. The remains of moustachios are faintly visible at either end of the bridge. Four panels of mother-of-pearl on the fingerboard are engraved with allegorical figures of Fire, Air, Water, and Earth. Andromeda and the sea monster are engraved on the upper head and a sleeping, unidentified nymph on the lower head. The full splendour of this instrument is seen when it is turned over to reveal the thirteen ebony flutes of the soundbox, inlaid with scrolling tendrils of ivory, sprouting leaves, and grotesque heads. The back of the neck is similarly inlaid with animals, satyrs, and humans, several making music with instruments of all kinds. Giorgio Sellas and his brother Matteo were instrument- makers of German origin, based in Venice, where they made a number of spectacularly decorated lutes and guitars in the first half of the seventeenth century.

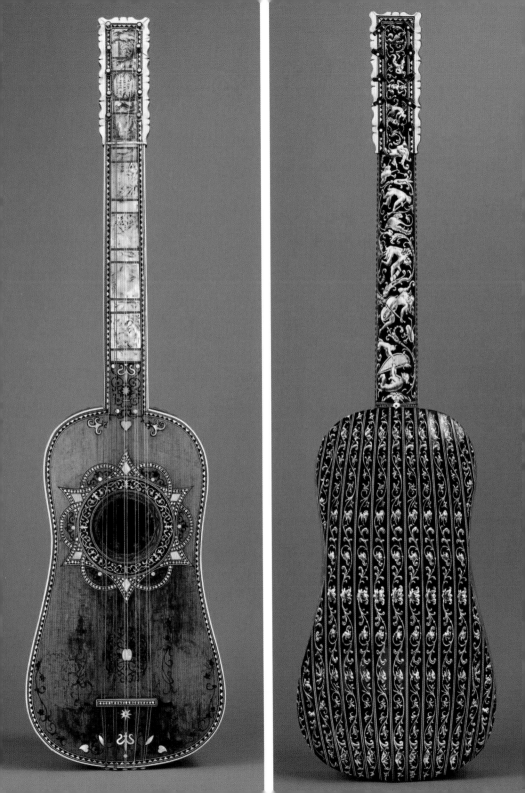

Guitar by René Voboam (c.1606–71)

incised on the face of the head:
René / Voboam / 1641

Length with neck: 937; length of body: 462; width of upper, middle and lower bouts: 205, 183, 246; max. depth of sides: 88; string length: 696.

Topham, 1627
Boyden, no. 40
Presented by W. E. Hill & Sons, 1939

Boyden first correctly read the maker's name as René Voboam, the founder of a dynasty of French guitar-makers in seventeenth- and eighteenth-century Paris. The front is made of uncoloured, close-grained soft-wood, either pine or spruce: it is difficult to be sure, as the endgrain that distinguishes the two is hidden by the inlay. The rose is made of four ornate layers of paper set within a retaining ring of ivory and an outer ring of alternating ebony and ivory. The same pattern of ebony and ivory runs along the contours of the front, on the side of the neck and on the bridge. The ends of the bar sprout neat moustachios inlaid with flowerheads of ivory. A scrolling foliate design in ivory decorates the ebony face of the fingerboard. The back and sides are inlaid in a chevron pattern of tortoiseshell with inset quatrefoils of mother-of-pearl arranged in a diamond pattern in the centre. A related pattern of tightly serried chevrons in ebony, ivory, and mother-of-pearl is skilfully inlaid into the back of the neck. The head, lightly angled, has ten ebony pegs, inlaid with ebony and mother-of-pearl, inserted from behind, carrying five double courses. This is one of only four instruments attributed to Voboam: all are similarly dec-orated with the same striking combination of tortoise-shell and mother-of-pearl.

Guitar by Antonio Stradivari (1644?–1737)

signed with inlay on the back of the head: *ANT:^{S} STRADIVARIUS / CREMONEN^S:S F. 1688*

length with neck: 1,004; length of body: 470; width of upper, middle, and lower bouts: 215, 178, 110; max. depth of sides: 105; string length: 741.

Topham, 1654
Boyden, no. 41
Presented by W. E. Hill & Sons, 1939

Guitars by Stradivari are extremely rare. If we take into consideration the patterns in the Cremona museum, he must have made more than we realize, but only one other complete guitar, now in the Shrine to Music Museum in South Dakota, is known to survive along with some fragments, including a neck in the Paris Conservatoire. The refined simplicity of the Ashmolean instrument contrasts with the exuberance of some other seventeenth-century guitars. The rose, beautifully designed and cut from dark brown fruitwood, is set within a circle of mother-of-pearl squares and lozenges, similar to those found on Stradivari's inlaid violins. The uncoloured softwood front is edged with ebony, and there is a little leaf-shaped inset of ebony at the centre of the lower edge. The bridge at one time carried curling moustachios that have left a faint trace on the surface of the wood. The back is made from four lengths of golden maple, separated by lines of black inlay. The pegbox is veneered with ebony with two strips of bone inlay to match the fingerboard. Bone strips run down the sides of the fingerboard. Originally these strips went only as far as the end of the ebony veneer, but then Stradivari (or a later restorer) continued them to the shoulders. In general, the guitar has survived in excellent condition, although an inscription inside the instrument on one of the strengthening bars: *Rep. W.J. 1914*, discovered by Stephen Barber in 1978, suggests that it has been opened and repaired at least once. On the wood below the ebony of the fingerboard is an incised blank shield, supported by putti, which is probably purely ornamental. Ten strings in five double

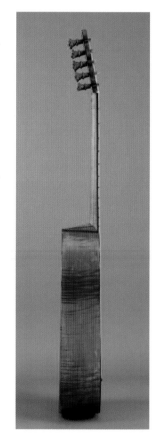

courses are tuned by pegs inserted at the rear of the head. The eighteen metal frets, which have been inserted into the fingerboard and continue down the front, are probably not original. Guitar frets in this period were normally made of gut. A series of little dents along the neck on the treble side suggest that this guitar, also, was at one time fitted with gut frets.

Guitar by Antonio dos Santos Vieira (early eighteenth century)

label: *Antonio / dos S^{tos} Viéyra / a feze ïm / l x a;* inscribed in pen on an oval paper label gummed down within a decorative cartouche painted on the back in greenish-blue, pink, and white body colours

length with neck: 970; length of body: 464; width of upper, middle, and lower bouts: 228, 190, 290; max. depth of sides: 94; string length: 681.

Topham, 1684
Boyden, no. 42
Presented by W. E. Hill & Sons, 1939.

This is an early eighteenth-century instrument, wider at the bouts and flatter at the top than the other guitars in the Ashmolean. The sound-hole has no rose, but it is set within a rosette ornament inlaid with eye-like motifs of ivory. This eye motif reappears on the finger-board, along the sides, on the stringbar, and on the head. Moustachios flow outwards from the bridge in a filigree design inlaid with little dots of ivory like tiny fruit scattered through the branches of a tree. The back and sides are made of a rich dark tropical hardwood, against which the white ivory inlay, elegantly designed in the form of three looping cords, is strikingly empha-sized. The head, which is long and steeply angled, is grafted onto the neck, perhaps for the sake of saving wood. The heel, also, is built up in three parts. Twelve ivory pegs, decorated with black dots, carry six double courses, which are fixed lopsided to the string bar and have been reconfigured. Two of the string holes are larger than the others, and the last hole on the bass side has been added. Originally, it must have had five courses, gathered in two triple strings and three double. The frets are missing, but the impress of gut frets is faintly visible on the neck. The elaborately decorated label translates: 'Antonio dos Santos Vieira made this in Lisbon.'

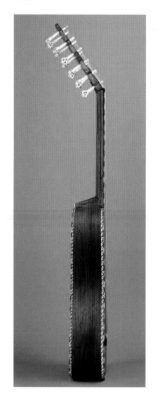

English guitar by John N. Preston (working 1734–70)

stamped on the base of the peg-box: *PRESTON MAKER / LONDON* below a crowned monogram of the maker's initials.

length with neck: 736; length of body: 356; width: 292; max. depth of sides: 70; string length: 420

Topham, 1692
Boyden, no. 35
Presented by A. Phillips Hill in accordance with the wishes of Arthur and Alfred Hill, 1948.

The English guitar – or 'guittar', as it was often spelled at the time – is not a guitar but a late variant of the cittern. The form may have been introduced from Germany at the time of the Hanoverian succession, but it developed into a particularly British instrument, very popular with amateurs in fashionable society. The soundboxes of the two instruments by Preston in the Ashmolean are typical of his work. The front of this guitar is made of softwood, varnished golden brown, with a twelve-pointed rose of ebony and ivory set in an open-work ornament of polished wood. The back and sides are made of varnished maple, outlined with pen and ink in place of inlaid purfling. It has six courses of strings (four double) and a device called a capotasto, a bar, tightened by a nut against the neck, that can stop the strings in four positions in order to raise or lower the pitch by a semitone. The heads of both instruments are inlaid with a starburst of ivory and dark wood. The main difference between the two is in the tuning system, which is operated in this guitar with ten rosewood pegs, probably original, whereas the head of its companion is fitted with a mechanical device invented by Preston and widely adopted by rival makers.

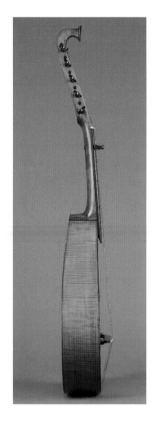

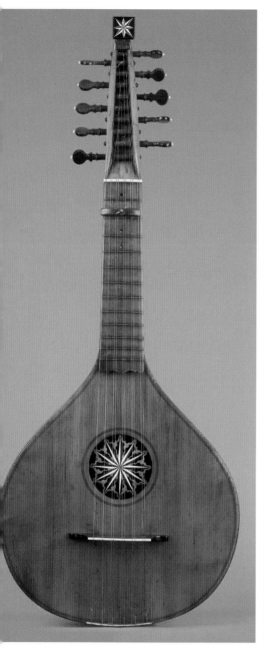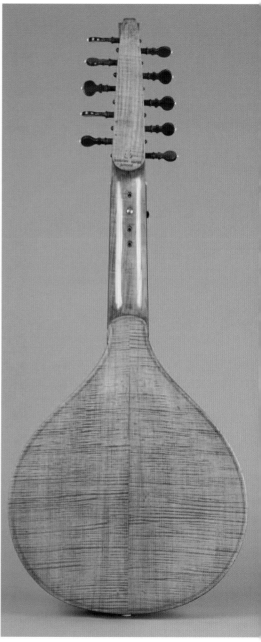

English guitar by John N. Preston (working 1734–70)

stamped on the back of the head:
PRESTON MAKER / LONDON
below a crowned monogram of the maker's initials

length with neck: 678; length of body: 355; width: 292; max. depth of sides: 68; string length: 422.

Topham, 1719
Boyden, no. 34
Presented by A. Phillips Hill in accordance with the wishes of Arthur and Alfred Hill, 1948

There are four penlines instead of three round the rose-hole, but, otherwise, the soundbox of this instrument is almost identical to the soundbox of its companion. Both are strung with six courses of strings, the upper four double, and have twelve metal frets inset into the ebony fingerboard. The strings on this instrument, however, are tuned by means of a brass mechanism, invented by Preston, in which the tension is controlled by a watch-key inserted into a row of ten little holes in the head. These operate ten brass pegs, carrying the strings, which slide along ten vertical slots in the face of the machine. The mechanism is inscribed: *PRESTON INVENTOR* below the tuning: *CEGCEG*. The head grafted onto the neck is sickle-shaped in order to give access to the keyholes. This is an ingenious device, which prevents the strings going slack by accident and gives a fine degree of control over the short wire strings. These are strung over an ivory saddle on the lower edge and are fixed to ten ivory pins in the base above an ivory button, which may have been inserted to protect the pins from damage.

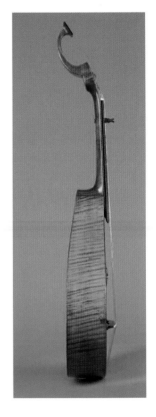

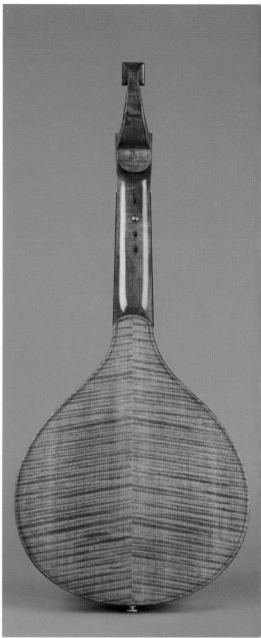

English guitar by Michael Rauche (working c.1758–c.1770)

inscribed in ink on the button:
Rauche / London: 1770

length with neck: 790; length of body: 359; width: 302; max. depth of sides: 73; string length: 485.

Topham, 1750
Boyden, no. 36
Presented by A. Phillips Hill in accordance with the wishes of Arthur and Alfred Hill, 1948.

Michael Rauche belonged to a group of instrument-makers of German origin working in eighteenth-century London. In the late 1750s he had a partner called Hoffman but had set up on his own in Chandos Street by 1762. The soundbox of this ornate instrument is pear-shaped with indented sides. It has a softwood front, and the back and sides are made of bird's eye maple, the back in two finely matched pieces separated by a strip of inlay. There are similar strips of inlay along the edges of the sides and head. The front and back are edged with ivory. The rose is formed from a twelve-pointed star, inlaid with mother-of-pearl, tortoiseshell, and brown wood, set within two outer rings of tortoiseshell. Two further rings have been added in pen and ink. The finger board is veneered with tortoiseshell, inlaid with engraved plaques of mother-of-pearl. It has six double courses, regulated by twelve metal ring-headed keys inserted laterally that turn frontal spindels by means of a rachet mechanism. The strings are fixed at the lower end to ivory pins above an ivory button, inlaid with mother-of-pearl. The neck has a capotasto with holes for four positions and twelve metal frets.

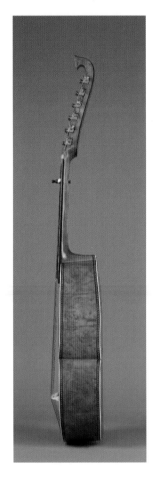

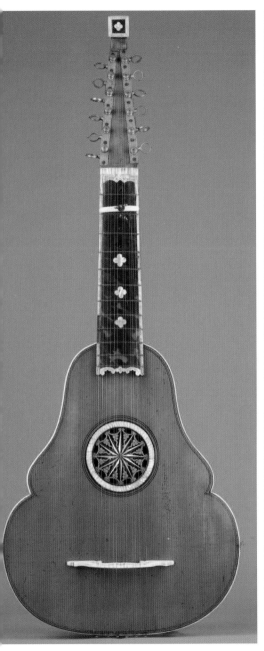
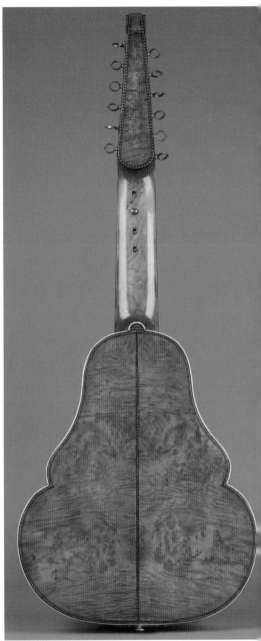

English guitar by Frederick Hintz (d. 1772)

Impressed on the back of the neck and again on the top of the back: *F. HINTZ*; the same inscription is cast in the metal rose.

length with neck: 700; length of body: 355; width: 310; max. depth of sides: 79; string length: 412.

Boyden, no. 37
Presented by A. Phillips Hill in accordance with the wishes of Arthur and Alfred Hill, 1948.

Hintz specialized in making guitars. He had an address in Leicester Fields and is described in the London Universal Directory of 1763 as 'Guitar maker to His Majesty and to the Royal Family'. In common with most instruments of this kind, the front and two-piece maple back of this instrument have been outlined in pen and ink. The rose of gilt cast brass is also a common type, ornamented with a winged boy, holding a long garland within an outer band of instruments, which include four coiled hunting horns. The soundbox is varnished dark brown, and the fingerboard, veneered with red tortoiseshell, is inlaid and edged with mother-of-pearl. The head, which has been fitted with a watch-key mechanism, is inscribed in pen and ink below the slotted plate: *Prestons New / Instrument / [- -] 31 1786*. On account of this, the instrument has been generally dated 1786. Hintz, however, died in 1772, and the date inserted on the head probably records the time when the instrument was altered to install the tuning mechanism. The upper neck and the sickle-shaped head have been joined to the base of the neck by means of a long diagonal graft. The clumsy placing of the capotasto holes, cut partly through the ornament of the neck and set off-centre (as they usually are to avoid interfering with the strings), suggests that they were not part of the original design.

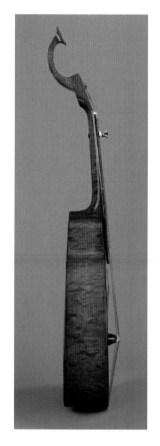

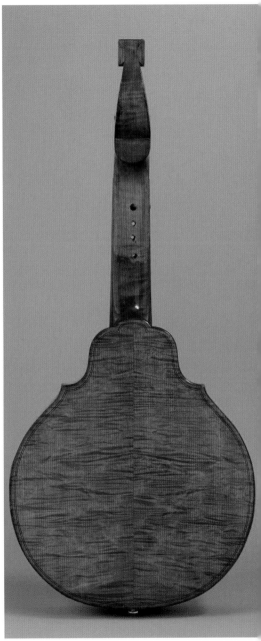

English guitar by Lucas (late eighteenth century)

Little is known about Lucas. According to his trade card, he had premises at the Golden Guitar in Little Newport Street and 'makes and teaches ye Guittar in the Completest manner'. The gilt brass rose, with its retaining ring of ivory, is ornamented with a putto playing a trumpet within a band of instruments very similar to the rose on Hintz's guitar. Roses of this kind must have been supplied to makers by a common source. The softwood front, outlined with a single line in pen and black ink, has been damaged, perhaps by damp, and has been varnished dark brown. The sides and two-piece back of maple are similarly varnished. The tortoiseshell veneer on the neck is also very dark. The ivory bridge is edged with scrolls and incised with a blackened diaper pattern. There are thirteen frets. The strings are fitted to ten pegs of dark-stained wood, gathered in five double courses and fixed at the base to nine ivory pins and one nail (in place of a missing pin). There is a graft about a third of the way along the neck from the soundbox. To judge from its present condition, it has not always been well cared for.

printed label: *Lucas at ye Golden / Guittar Silver Street / Golden Square*

length with neck: 745; length of body: 348; width: 312; max. depth of sides: 76; string length: 414.

Boyden, no. 38
Presented by A. Phillips Hill in accordance with the wishes of Arthur and Alfred Hill, 1948

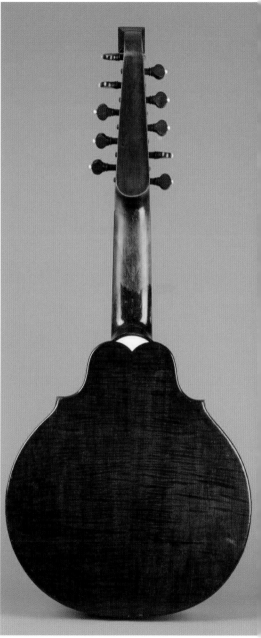

Technical Terms

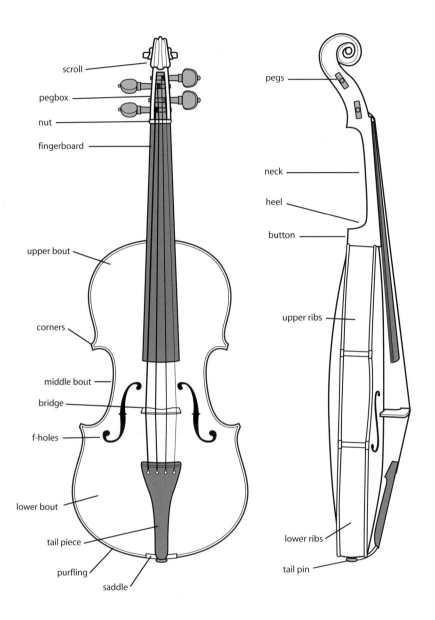

scroll

pegbox

nut

fingerboard

upper bout

corners

middle bout

bridge

f-holes

lower bout

tail piece

purfling

saddle

pegs

neck

heel

button

upper ribs

lower ribs

tail pin

Further Reading

Baines, Anthony, *Musical Instruments through the Ages* (London, 1966).

Boyden, David B., *The History of Violin Playing from its Origins to 1761* (London, 1965).

Boyden, David B., *The Hill Collection* (Oxford, 1969; 2nd edn., 1979).

Cacciatori, Fausto (ed.), *Andrea Amati Opera Omnia, Les Violons du Roi*, exhibition catalogue, Cremona, Museo Civico, 29 September–14 October 2007.

Cooper, Albert, *The Cooper Collection*, 2 vols. (Ashford, 1996, 1998).

Fleming, Michael, *Viol-Making in England c.1580–1660*, VME CD-Rom (Oxford, 2002).

Hargrave, Roger, 'Andrea Amati 1505–1577', *The Strad*, 102/1220 (December 1991), 1093–107.

Hill, W. E., & Sons, *The Salabue Stradivari* (London, 1891).

Peters, Joanna, *et al.*, *The Strad*, vol. 112/1312 (August 2001) (special edition).

Pollens, Stewart, *The Violin Forms of Antonio Stradivari* (London, 1992).

Topham, John, 'A Dendrochronological Survey of the Musical Instruments of the Cremonese School', *Journal of Archaeological Science*, 27 (2000), 183–92.

Topham, John, 'A Dendrochronological Survey of the Musical Instruments in the Hill Collection at the Ashmolean Museum, Oxford', *Galpin Society Journal*, 55 (April 2002), 244–68.

Witten, Laurence C., 'The Surviving Instruments of Andrea Amati', *Early Music*, 10/4 (1982), 487–94.

Woodfield, Ian, *The Early History of the Viol* (Cambridge, 1984).